POEMS OF ACCORD AND SATISFACTION

Poems and Pictures

By

JILL BAKER

A Winchester Cottage Print Book

A Winchester Cottage Print Book
Published by LSI
WinchesterCottage Print
A Division of Winchester Cottage Fine Art and Print
618 Main Street, #184
New Harmony, Indiana 47631

Cover design by Jill Baker
Illustrations by Jill Baker

All rights reserved. No part of this book may be reproduced or transmitted in any form or by any means, electronic or mechanical, including photocopying, recording, or by any information storage and retrieval system, without the written permission of the publisher, except where permitted by law. For information address Winchester Cottage Print, 618 Main Street, Suite 184, New Harmony, IN 47631

Printed in the United States of America

Copyright 2009

Poems of Accord and Satisfaction
Table of Contents

	Page
ACCIDENT	1
BABY FOOL	2
WHY WALTZ?	4
THE WAKE (THE WAIT)	6
BRIM	8
CALIFORNIA AFTERNOON	12
COMING STORM	13
CONVERSATION ON A COUNTRY ROAD	15
CRASH SITE (4 POEMS)	18
DECEMBER	22
DREAM DANCER	23
I FELT ETERNITY END	29
FEBRUARY	31
FUSCIA PETALS	34
I AM THIS LEAF	35
JANUARY	38
LIES	39
LOVER (AFTER POE)	41
LUXURY	43
TAKE IT FROM ME	45
VACATION	48
NATURAL DANCER	49
MY BABY'S SMILE: (TO BETSY)	51
NEGLECT	53
ONCE	54
TO BE SPOKEN WITH A SOUTHERN ACCENT	57
TELL HER	59
WHEN PARADISE CLOSED	61
REQUEST	63
WHERE IS LIFE?	63
THE PERFECT POEM	64

ACCIDENT

The deer still hangs, just beyond the windshield
Suspended over the hood of my car
Her tail high and white,
Her long body mottled gray with brown here and there,
Her front legs white and
Stretched out before her,
The slender hind legs with delicate gray hooves
Carefully folded up under her,
Ears up on her bony head
Large black eyes looking not at me,
But toward the far side of the road
Where she wills to be.

Still as a star
She hangs in the air.

I close my eyes,
But she remains.

BABY FOOL

(You left me in the café, drunk and feelin' low,
Crying like a baby. Now here's my song of woe:)

Baby Fool, Baby Fool, I'm a sucker, as a rule
Falling for your kind of cruel,
Forgetting things I learned in school.
Baby, I'm your Baby Fool.

How you've changed, it makes me dizzy
Now that you're no lover,
You say that you are very busy,
But it's just a cover.

You take me out and leave me sittin'
Wonderin' 'bout the love I'm gettin'
If I'd known sooner, I'd be cool,
But Baby, I'm your Baby Fool.

Baby Fool, Baby Fool,
I'm a sucker, as a rule
Falling for your kind of cruel,
Forgetting things I learned in school.
Baby, I'm your Baby Fool.

You treat me bad, you treat me cruel
You treat me lowdown as a rule.
Now they see me sit and cry,
Chew my nails and act a fool
Baby, I'm your Baby Fool.

WHY WALTZ?

Why waltz when you can be lonely?
Why waltz when you can be blue?
You ask me why that I'm only
Happy when I waltz with you.
Well. . .

You ask me why and I tell you
You ask me to dance and I do
There's no turning round when you're waltzing
I'll dance only one waltz,
Or two,
Well. . .

Why waltz when you can be lonely?
Why waltz when you can be blue?
And you ask me why that I'm only
Happy when I waltz with you.

THE WAKE
(The Wait)

The earth gashed red
Before the winter snows
Lie brazen on her open wounds.
Aging symmetry
Of silver board
And rusting roofs.

Scratch-marks
From some idle hand
Etched branches on the metal sky.
Amber memories and
Flutterings turned black
Upon a still gray earth
Wait, shivering
On the tips of brittle grass
For the bitter frost.
Flocks across the quiet skies
Flee winds
Which wail on winter nights.

BRIM

Brim coffee and I'm wearing my new blue dress
In the morning.
While I walk down the hall
Carpet past the secretarial stations
With computers humming,
Some smiling lips
Look up to see me,
Friendly but busy, busy.

Morning means the mail arrives;
I get the knife
I open some man's envelopes,
Get my fingers black,
Stamp the date on the stiff white unfolding papers,
Make notes; put the crinkled pile on his desk,
Important stuff on top, junk on the bottom.
Can't throw out the junk, it may be important.

Silence--I sit
In front of the green screen,

Beeps and hums from warm machines surround me,
Time has no meaning in the morning
Get the job done and it does get done.
My mind drifts away from the little words on the screen,
Out the window.

His love comes and goes
It comes and goes in my mind.
It is in my mind that it comes and goes,
Not his.
He loves me.
It is my mind where the leaves wash around
And up and down on the green surface.
He loves me with his body, he loves me – or
Does he love me with his mind?
Once he did.

He comes and goes.
He leaves after a long time.
He comes back after a long time.
He loves me, he leaves me.
I love him and I know him and I tolerate him.
His head back when he feels good,

His grin and the side glances
That mean he is thinking of me
And what do I think?

His body warm in the night
When we sleep and I wake and sleep
Feeling his leg on mine.
The smooth skin of his back
In the morning, pressing my breasts on him,
He hums like my machine does now
In the morning, waking with me.

His hair, curled just right,
The shirt he wears all the time.
He is proud,
A man with a temper and over other men.
He has to have his way.
He has his way with me.
He thinks I am sweet, and I am.

He walks in,
Cold and proud
And begins to talk.

We talk side by side.
He brushes my arm when I talk
And then he kisses me,
Leaning his head down to touch my hair.

I'm sweet as coffee in the morning.
I love him in the night, sweet as sugar.
Giving him sugar
Calling him darling.
He is sweet to me in his pride.

Brim coffee--cold and sweet.
I am swinging in my work,
Time to talk to the boss,
Time to eat lunch,
Time to talk to the secretaries.
Brim in the morning and Brim at 3.
Running down the hall at 5:05
To copy the documents,
Ripping the Federal Express form out,
Running across the street to mail it.
It is time to go to him at last.

CALIFORNIA AFTERNOON

It's a California afternoon
Like all other ones.
Twin cat eyes stare at me
From under the bougainvillea,
And beside the green lawn
The red poinsettias
Bloom against the palm.
Dark glasses on, in my hammock
In the shade,
I sleep and read.
The sun burns white
Behind my eyes,
Throwing darts of light
From the blue pool.
Figs hang over me,
Black and withered.
Old men's balls.
It's a California afternoon
After all.

COMING STORM

The sky is cloudy, heavy, dark.
A storm is blowing from the South.
The wind is wailing, the dogs bark.
The cats crouch, waiting in the house
They hear approaching thunder, rain,
And see the lightning in the night.

We wait in silence, wait in pain,
Dreading a hurtful, angry fight.
We do not look, no longer seek
Words like "love you" when we part.
We say "Be careful," we don't speak
Of things real in our heart.
It can't be long before the brunt
Of broken torrents flow
In the thunder and the flash
Of lightning strikes, when cold winds blow.

The dogs are anxious, coveting love.
I understand, I feel their pain,
And under darkening skies above,
Receive their kisses in the rain.

CONVERSATION ON A COUNTRY ROAD

"You see that cloud, just sittin' yonder in the sky?
All glowy around the edges
Like Jesus was sittin' in it?
You know, sometimes I wonder
If the time isn't closer than we think.
The world can't last much longer,
The way it's goin'. . .

"Why, this last month
A friend of mine
Was beaten to death. . .
Beaten   to   death, can you imagine?
Head bashed in—eyes knocked out,
Until he died
So the undertaker had to build his face all back
To let the casket be open.
Done in by a gang in Detroit.
It's the Godawful truth!

"It says Jesus is comin' in a cloud, don't it?
That's what the Bible says.
I was just wonderin',
Hearin' voices
Down the road, kinder soundin' like
They was a long way off,
If Jesus isn't just sittin' in that cloud,
Hummin' with the angels,
And maybe cleaning his fingernails,
Because he's bout ready to come back,
And anxious to get the whole mess over with."

CRASH SITE (4 Poems)

My eyes are giving me trouble
Tears flow for no reason.
Where did it go, my heart?
And you write me, "No,
You cannot see me."
You have your life and I have mine.
We flew in parallel slots
Down effluent lanes of air,
Far apart forever.
But similar patterns we formed
Throughout our lives.
We saw the sky above,
The earth alike.
Where shall I dwell, if not with you?
Our spirits are one.

We fly abreast
Both drenched in morning mist,
One eye,
One soul,

One way to live.
On wings of wire
Across the lines of space
We talked and loved.
By night and day.
Eons we crossed before we met.
Fire flew when we met
We did not miss, yet
I continue to fly.
Where did you go?
Did you crash and burn?
Do you still
Deny we touched?
Have you not the heart for such?
Your wings fly not with mine.
If you still fly
We fly apart.

My wings beat like a heart.
My tears a river make
This water the way
I find my path.
Above it all we fly

Flowing in streams across the sky
A river rushing dark
Horizon to horizon,
One can only see
A wave of wings
Unable to stop, or flee,
I fly.

I feared I'd left you,
Asked my soul,
As I passed by,
And heard the noise,
And saw the light,
Am I still whole,
Or did I leave you
Downed, at the crash site?

DECEMBER

He comes no more
The short days long
I see the end of the year
No glory in winning
No sating in tears
He is not there to know or hear
I feel no press or praise
When all is silent in my life
How still it is when I don't hear
The He no longer near.

DREAM DANCER

We're a couple of wisened old swans,
Aren't we, my Dream Dancer? You and I –
We've stood in our corners and toughed it out, haven't we?
Watching the one we love flirt with other dancers,
Pretending we don't care, you and I.
We've gone through that a million times
On the floor and in our minds,
Each time wondering if we could survive this one.
And not feel again those old feelings of despair.
You stood there
In the door, in your dress shirt,
Watching me with some young man,
I saw your heart
Breaking through the metal buttons,
Shining in your tuxedo, with your red bow tie
All the way across the room.
How I hated you
Floating away with some new young woman
With which I can't compete.
I've given it up again and again
I gave up my heart, each time I saw you

You dream dancer, you,
Shining in your red shirt and black hat,
Gazing across the dance floor at
Me shining with my hair dyed gold
And some new dress,
Dying for the chance
To win some young man's dance.

We're a pair of wise ones, aren't we my old Dream dancer?
Too wise.
We toughed it out till it's too late
I hear you call each night
When it's too late, about what went on before.
When you, my dream dancer, went dancing
Into the dark with a young, pink, chiffon skirt.
Calling me because you don't know why
You love me tonight more than you knew.
You didn't know you had it in you
My tough old darling,
Standing before me in the morning
With your wrinkles showing me,
My wrinkles showing you,
We aren't quite so young any more.

When will we learn, my old dream dancer?
We glow like a neon sign
Together, spelling love
To the world that sees us loving
All the world tells me you love me
All but you tell me you love me
All but you love me
My dream dancer,
I dance for those
Who love me,
Dance for you,
Wait for you, to dance with me
Wait for you to
Dream for dances with
Dancing for dreams with
You, my old
Dream dancer

We don't know why we tough it out
Do we?
Dance every night, to dream
For a moment
Of the strength and beauty

We hold in our arms, the shining eyes

Of the young, we are young

And hopeful again

For a moment.

We dance forever young in the fresh, strong arms

Of our dreams

You and I

Dance until we forget

Until our feet ache

And our bones ache

And our faces are full of creases

And the truth comes back to us

In the cold restroom mirror.

We are not young.

We have danced a million dances.

We are alike

You and I

We'll dance until

Our love is lost

In chiffon skirts

And strong young arms in cotton shirts.

Dance, dream lover
Is the only lover that hasn't proven fickle,
Like all our lovers
Like we to all our lovers.

Will we love again --
Can we love again each other?
After all those lovers
Who danced away with our hearts
When we were young and not so tough?
My darling Dancer,
Standing there alone in a black dress suit
In the semi-dark,
King and beggar,
Gazing at me dancing,
Knowing
Across the floor,
Moving,
We love.

I FELT ETERNITY END

In the beginning you were there
The sun shone in your eyes
Our love was true,
Our world was fair
And true love never died

They say love lasts forever
That true love never dies
The stars will always shine above
The sun will always rise

But nothing lasts for always
One day the sun won't rise
The moon and stars won't shine above
Your eyes will not meet mine.

I thought the stars and moons remained
When everything else was gone
I thought the universe infinite
But nothing lasts that long.

Don't tell me that our love is dead
And now we are just friends.
You turned your eyes and hid the sun,
I felt eternity end.

The light is gone from your loving eyes
My day turns into night
They say all things must come to an end
And even the sun will die.

FEBRUARY

(While sitting in the waiting room of an oncologist)

I see the Monet paintings
Of girls in grass beneath the summer trees
And realize it is not yet spring.
Yet I would, if I could,
Fling myself down wholeheartedly upon that grass
And hold the damp earth close to me,
Breathing in the fragrance of crushed daisies,
Water cress and fresh young plants,
Turning and looking up through the leaves
Just budding above,
To blue unbounded air.

I know I soon will float into those empty spaces
My atoms mingling with those that also bear
Feathers, gossamer wings and warm sun rays.
But now I look through frosted glass
To see dark mud and chilling puddles
Beneath bare limbs
And would hold them close, too
If I could but stay till spring.

FUSCIA PETALS

Fuscia petals in a spider web
Fly in the wind on invisible strings
Free, yet caught
How could there be
A tie so strong, unseen?

I AM THIS LEAF

I am this leaf,
Veins extended, colors bright,
That lies upon my windowsill this night.
Its dry frame resembles mine.
Soon it too will crack and shatter
Upon the white sheet it lies upon
I know, because it is I
Who will be pieces no one can put together
My life will no longer resemble me
Though I am remembered.

I've seen how images change
When death has laid its hand
Upon a life.
Those who remain work feverishly,
To reconstruct, retain
Those things left
In memory and on paper
There's no way to reconcile
The strange with the known.

My colors entertain

My images remain

Yet when I crumble into dust

And am swept away,

There will be no one left

Who can put me together again.

JANUARY

I tried to tell him with a poem,
But he said he didn't understand my poetry.
I'm trying to understand life,
And he's trying to understand why I want him
To pay the rent.
I'm trying to get my life together
To accomplish something,
He's trying to make love
And guess what I do?

LIES

It was evening and the cars were honking.
I had a sinking feeling.
I was sinking through the pavement.
My life sinking—through the pavement.
I had thought too much and realized he lied.

Everyone lies.
The one I trusted most had lied to me --
So had others during my life.
But I wished his lies into truth.
I trusted his and hoped to make them true.
But he tried to lie his way out of his lies,
And that's how I knew.

I trusted the pavement to hold me up.
But even the pavement was in disguise.
It swallowed me up.
Right through the concrete I went
With all my white packages.
Chunks of sidewalk floated up past me.

Faces watched me as I sank,
Mouths open in amazement.

Somehow I felt relieved.
Somehow the truth was out.
The truth was out
And I was taken in.

LOVER
(After Poe)

Late last night as I lay dreaming,
Searching for a lighted door.
'Round about me there was darkness,
Seeming ever more –
I could not stop the tears that poured
For my dear lover came no more.

Once I lived, but for me only --
With no lover, being lonely
In the dark recesses of my mind,
When my dear love,
He came to find.

I was bathed in warm caresses,
Bound about with silken tresses
In and out the dark recesses
Of my mind the waters wind –
And my sweet love
He comes to mind.

I thought I lived--But without love?
Did he break the spell, I wonder?
When I found him, songs and laughter,
Kisses kind and sweet dreams after--
Were spells my sweet love
Brought me under.

Evil curses last as long as
There's no one to sing a song.
I shall love him though I'm lonely
Break the spell--I long to tell him,
When my sweet love, he
Comes to mind.

I slept, I dreamt,
Until I met him,
Saw his face and can't forget him,
Till he woke me up with music
Bringing happy day-dreams to me
O my dear Love is on my mind.

LUXURY

The feel of a warm cat lying
Silken, against my bare skin
Beneath a thin sheet
On a warm night
Just after I've bathed,
With my fragrant hair
Drying clean and curling,
My feather-soft pillow
Soft beneath my cheek,
While the man I love lies
Asleep in peace beside me.

TAKE IT FROM ME

Nothing about me is temporary,
Lovin' and leavin' aren't my cup of tea,
I'm not hard, Honey, I'm not contary.
I'm easy, Honey, take it from me
Take it, love, take it, love,
Take it from me.

Yes, I have suffered some heartache and pain,
When tears in my eyes and good-byes have burned,
I don't commiserate, I don't complain,
I just say it's a lesson I've learned.
Take it, love, take it, love,
Take it from me.

When heartaches and troubles flood over me,
And I feel like I'm washed out to sea,
I keep my heart safe and I keep my heart free,
I just want someone to take it from me.
Take it, love, take it, love,
Take it from me.

Can't you, my Honey, take it from me?
Believe me now, that I'm worth the keeping,
Don't be afraid, Honey, it's only me,
Wake up the love in a heart that's been sleeping.
Make it, love, make it, love,
Make it with me.

VACATION

Like the pain that remains
When you stop banging your head against the wall,
I sit, devoid of pressure, except for a small head-ache,
Among giant flowers in a white city on a hill,
It is the wind whistling below—not traffic,
That light is not neon,
Burning holes in my eyes.

The sound of children
Hawking toys hung on strings,
The cry of birds
The smell of hot foods frying
This is no longer work,
This is not my office
And I no longer exist.

NATURAL DANCER

I'm a natural dancer
I follow where you lead
I'm a natural mother
I'm sorry when you bleed.

I love to move, so move me
I love to love, so love me.

I'm a sweet romancer
I feel sorry for myself
Life's one big soap opera
On the TV on my shelf.

I'm a natural dancer
I follow where you lead
I'm a natural lover
And love is what I need.

I'm a natural dancer
Why should I dance on my own?
I think I dance much better
With a partner,
Not alone.

MY BABY'S SMILE:
(TO BETSY)

I glimpse in your smile
The remnants of my past.
A butterfly-flower day
Of babyhood and tender, mortal flesh. . .

Life passes in your smile.
The dimples become a crease,
A wrinkle in age.

One day I'll lie only
In your memory,
A rainbow fading
In the clouds
That fill your mind.

But in my memory you will stay;
As I pass into time,
A book, a photo, fading
Will bring to me your baby smile.

NEGLECT

All winter the dead leaves of the plant
Hung frozen on the dark porch,
Reminding me that I forgot
To bring it in
Before November's frost.
I heard it whisper,
Distraught,
Through black December nights,
In January it cried to me,
In the whining winds, with frenzied dance,
Its gray and trailing limbs;
Rattled, stiff and clacking,
Sheathed with silver February ice.
Its bare stalks shook under spring rains,
Branches gone, vanished leaves.
Till one warm day I rid it
Finally of its few frail bones,
Planted fresh seedlings in its dry bed,
And offered up new life to hang
Where damning wintry whispers once were heard.

ONCE

Once I was with you
Once I knew you
Once I touched you
Now I only remember
And dream unremembered dreams —
Of life and liberty,
Loving you.

I may get beyond that shell
You've wrapped around you,
Skillfully, on every side,
Cut the carefully constructed cover
You carry.
You have pierced mine
So many times.

Did you dream too?
Did your voice cry out my name
In the night?

I heard you.
I heard your voice so clearly
That I awoke in the early morning
Hearing you,
While everything was deathly still
And listened again.

TO BE SPOKEN WITH A SOUTHERN ACCENT

I sat on the front porch tonight
Waiting for Life to ride up on a big black horse.
His arms would glisten with sweat,
His coal-black hair would be sticking out
And he would carry the pitchfork of the devil in his hands.
But all that came along was the breeze,
Quiet, cooling, sweet with magnolias,
As the heat of the dead summer day
Throbbed from the silence of the night.

I sat on the front porch tonight
Waiting for Romance to prance by in size twelve shoes.
His beard would bristle brown against white teeth,
His broad shoulders could bear my weary head.
The strength of his arms in rolled-up sleeves
Would carry me off and I could be a girl again.
But all that came along was a neighbor's dog,
Snuffling the scent of invisible tracks,
His feet pattering in the dust,
And some fireflies blinking.

I sat on the front porch tonight

Waiting for Adventure to sweep me up in a silver plane.

Droning the night an oriental song.

Tomorrow I'd be flying over a blue, blue ocean.

And the folks back home would wonder where I'd gone.

But all I saw was the moon caught

In the needles of the pine tree,

And heard the song my baby sang through the window

To the first star in the night sky.

TELL HER

Tell her
Tell her
Tell her you love me
Tell her it's me that you adore.

Tell her
Tell her those kisses
You give her
Mean nothing any more.

Tell her
You're sorry, but
You meant it
When you made that vow.

Tell her
Tell her her smile
So sure, is wrong
And you love me now

Tell her
It's over, and
That sound that I'm hearing
Is her heart breaking —
Not mine.

WHEN PARADISE CLOSED

When Paradise closed
The other night
I felt a mild disappointment.
I had wanted so much to see it.

It sounded wonderful.
It had been something I had looked forward to seeing
Ever since I was a little girl
When I first heard them talking about it.

And then my grandmother,
Who had been there,
Described it to me.

It wasn't exactly what I had imagined,
But it sounded pretty good.
(At that time I would have preferred rock candy cobblestones to gold.)
But ah, the palaces, huge and cold,
As long as I didn't have to clean them,
Sounded better as I got old.

Oh, I knew I would have been bored
With nothing to do
In all that emptiness.

But at least I would be warmed
By the light of God's face.

I'm so sorry I won't get to see it now.
But as I've never seen it,
It's not too great a loss.

To have seen it and then lost it,
Would have been awful.

REQUEST

When I'm gone
Don't plant a stone.
Plant a tree,
Something live
That will survive
Long as the ghost of me.

WHERE IS LIFE?

Where is life
In the eyes or in the heart?
I know not which to choose on earth,
But up above, the life, all-knowing,
Many-named is where I'm going.
Art or Love – or both – may be my fate
If I but wait.

THE PERFECT POEM

The river ripples round in trickling tones
And all the little rattling river stones
Say one to another "You are my brother."

www.ingramcontent.com/pod-product-compliance
Lightning Source LLC
LaVergne TN
LVHW051512070426
835507LV00022B/3062